GROUNDWOOD BOOKS
HOUSE OF ANANSI PRESS
TORONTO BERKELEY

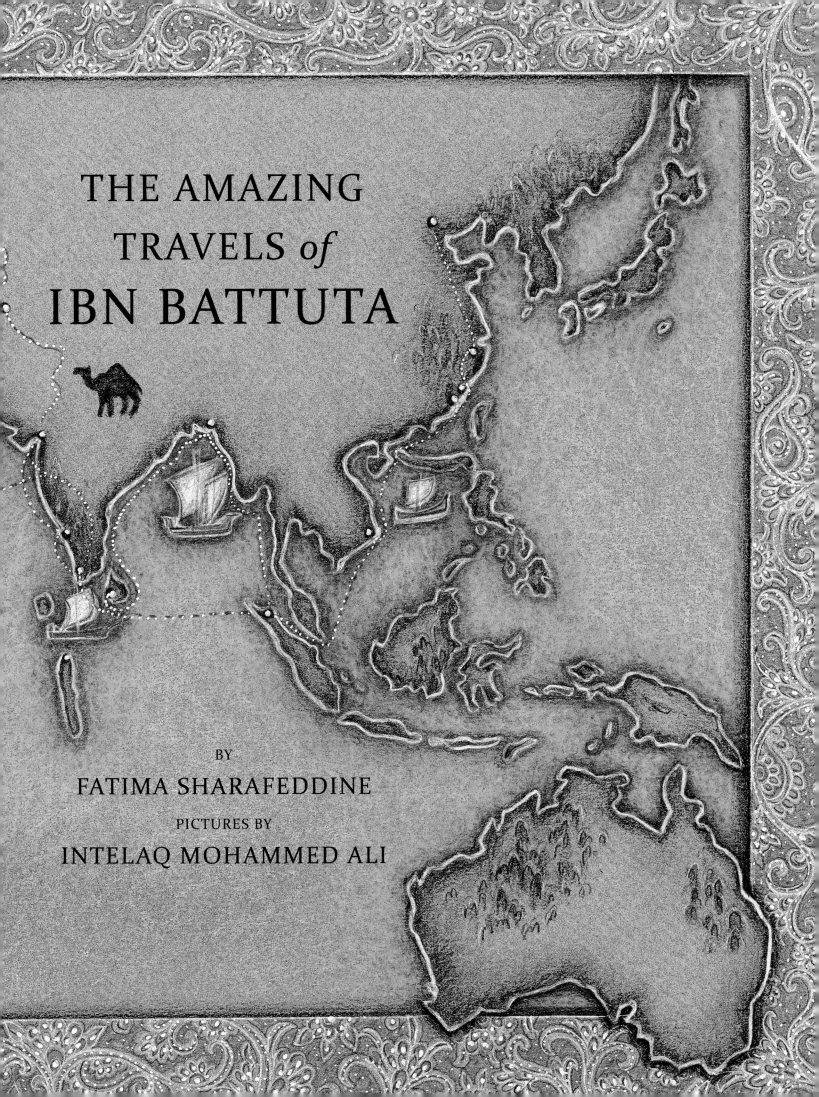

THE AMAZING TRAVELS of IBN BATTUTA

BY

FATIMA SHARAFEDDINE

PICTURES BY

INTELAQ MOHAMMED ALI

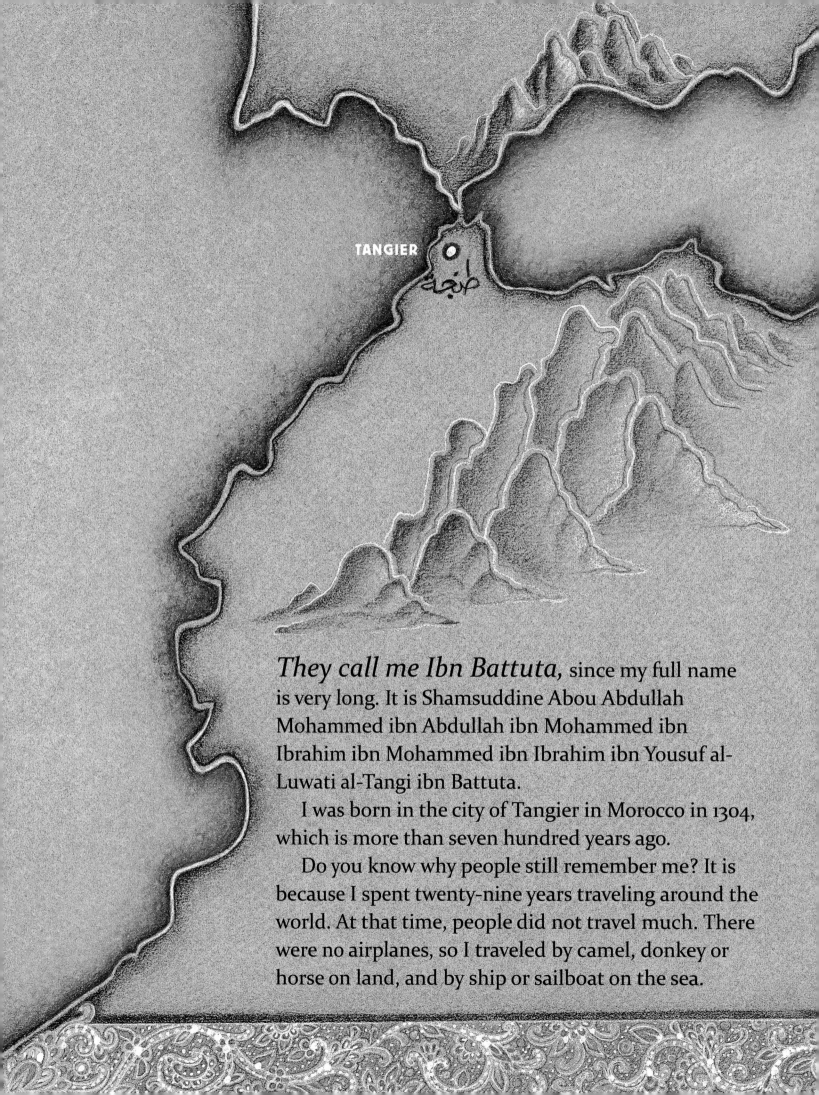

TANGIER

طنجة

They call me Ibn Battuta, since my full name is very long. It is Shamsuddine Abou Abdullah Mohammed ibn Abdullah ibn Mohammed ibn Ibrahim ibn Mohammed ibn Ibrahim ibn Yousuf al-Luwati al-Tangi ibn Battuta.

I was born in the city of Tangier in Morocco in 1304, which is more than seven hundred years ago.

Do you know why people still remember me? It is because I spent twenty-nine years traveling around the world. At that time, people did not travel much. There were no airplanes, so I traveled by camel, donkey or horse on land, and by ship or sailboat on the sea.

I set out on my first trip in 1325, when I was twenty-one years old. I wanted to go to Mecca, the holy city where the prophet Muhammad was born. My goal was to perform the pilgrimage, the Hajj. But I also loved the idea of visiting different places and meeting people from all over the world.

The day I said goodbye was very difficult for me and my parents, since we knew that traveling was full of dangers. I could be attacked by bandits, or face fierce sandstorms or dehydration in the desert. I started my trip alone on my donkey, but I soon met a caravan of merchants, so I joined them.

It took almost a year to get to Mecca. We went through Algeria, Tunisia, Libya, then Egypt and Syria. We finally arrived in 1326. I began my pilgrimage by walking seven times around the holiest site, the Kaaba. Once I had completed all the prayers and rituals, I stayed another three weeks visiting other holy places and meeting theologians.

On this first trip I got sick several times, but I always insisted on continuing my journey with the caravan no matter how I felt. During the long days of travel, we ate dried fruits such as dates, raisins and apricots. And since we had goats and sheep, we could eat meat and drink milk.

ALEXANDRIA

CAIRO

Upon entering a new city, I would introduce myself to its governors and religious leaders. They welcomed me warmly, listened to my stories about the lands I had seen, and offered me food and shelter. When I left, they gave me gifts and enough money to continue my travels, as was the custom.

Some of the cities that I visited charmed me with their beauty and liveliness. Alexandria fascinated me with its great seaport and famous lighthouse. Cairo impressed me with its mosques and hospitals.

JERUSALEM ©

But I did run into trouble from time to time. In Egypt, I had to fight off hyenas who attacked my bags and stole my supply of dates!

In Jerusalem, I visited the Dome of the Rock. I was first attracted by its amazing golden dome that shimmered from a distance. Gold covered the greater part of the inside as well, making it gleam and reflect light all over the place. I was astounded by the wonderful mosaic art and beautiful inscriptions from the Qur'an on the tiles. What a marvelous experience to pray in such a place!

This trip made me want to see the whole world. In 1326, I left Mecca with a caravan of pilgrims heading towards Persia, or Iran. I arrived in Isfahan where I remained for two weeks, meeting theologians and legal scholars.

Afterwards, I went to Shiraz and stayed there for a while. I slept in a dormitory connected to the mosque. I noticed that the people of Shiraz, especially the women, were very decent, kind and helpful. They also seemed to have a strong faith. Every Monday and Thursday, I saw a strange thing — about two thousand women would gather in the mosque to pray and worship God. I had never seen such a huge gathering of women in my life.

NAJAF

BASRA

BAGHDAD

NAJAF

It was 1327 by the time I continued my journey with a caravan to Baghdad, in Iraq. One of the customs in this city was to welcome strangers by inviting them to the public baths, the hammam, where they could wash with fragrant soaps in relaxing warm water. I greatly enjoyed the few hours that I spent there.

Then I went to Najaf to see the shrine of Imam Ali, the cousin and son-in-law of Prophet Muhammad.

After Najaf, I headed to Basra, a great Islamic city with a long history. It had the most important seaport in the region. When I arrived, I toured the city and prayed in its mosques, but did not stay for long.

BASRA

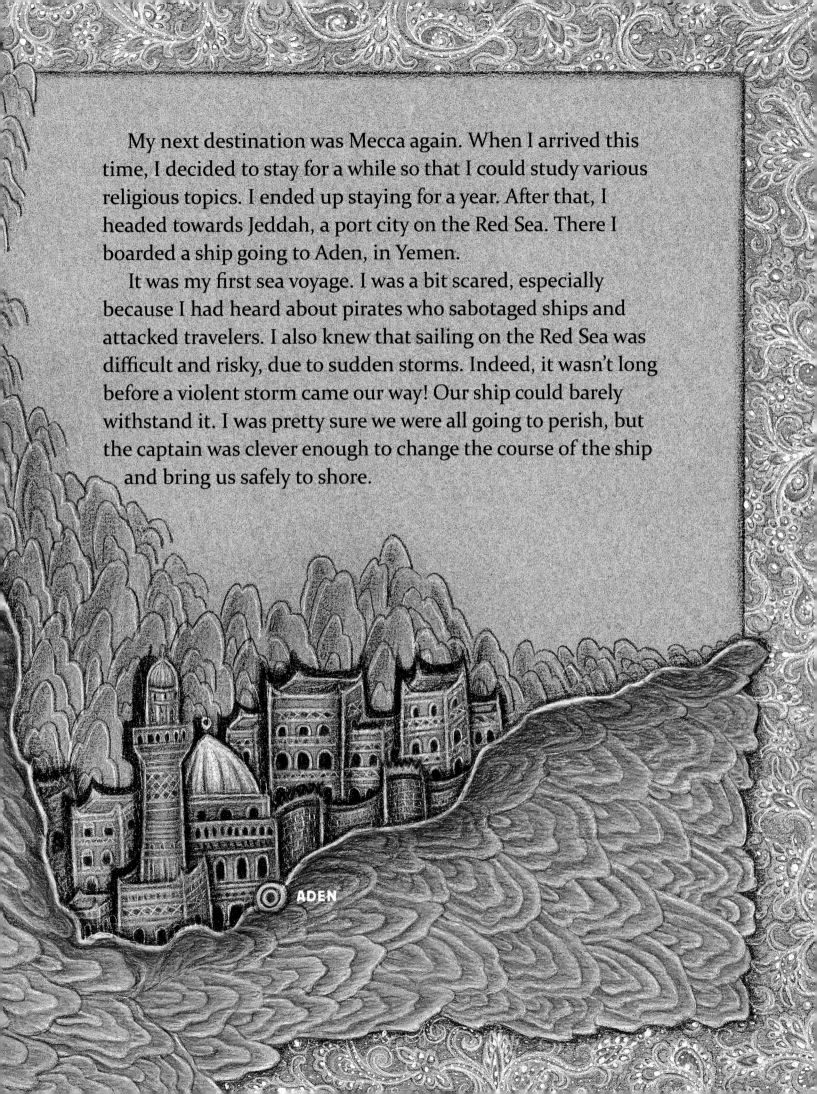

My next destination was Mecca again. When I arrived this time, I decided to stay for a while so that I could study various religious topics. I ended up staying for a year. After that, I headed towards Jeddah, a port city on the Red Sea. There I boarded a ship going to Aden, in Yemen.

It was my first sea voyage. I was a bit scared, especially because I had heard about pirates who sabotaged ships and attacked travelers. I also knew that sailing on the Red Sea was difficult and risky, due to sudden storms. Indeed, it wasn't long before a violent storm came our way! Our ship could barely withstand it. I was pretty sure we were all going to perish, but the captain was clever enough to change the course of the ship and bring us safely to shore.

ADEN

After that incident, I hired a camel to continue my journey.

In Yemen, I visited many coastal cities and mountainous villages. The king lived in Taiz, the biggest and most beautiful city in the country. I was told that he held a public hearing every Thursday. So I went to the palace the next Thursday and met with the qadi, the religious judge, who presented me to the king. I saluted him the way the qadi did. I touched the ground with my index finger, then lifted it to my head and said, "May God prolong thy Majesty."

The king ordered me to sit and questioned me about my country, the other lands I had visited and the rulers I had met. I stayed for a few days as his guest, and on the day of my departure, he offered me a horse.

I went on to Aden, to visit its seaport. There I saw merchant ships coming from the south carrying all kinds of goods — fruits, medicinal herbs, spices, dyes, iron, cotton, pearls, ivory...

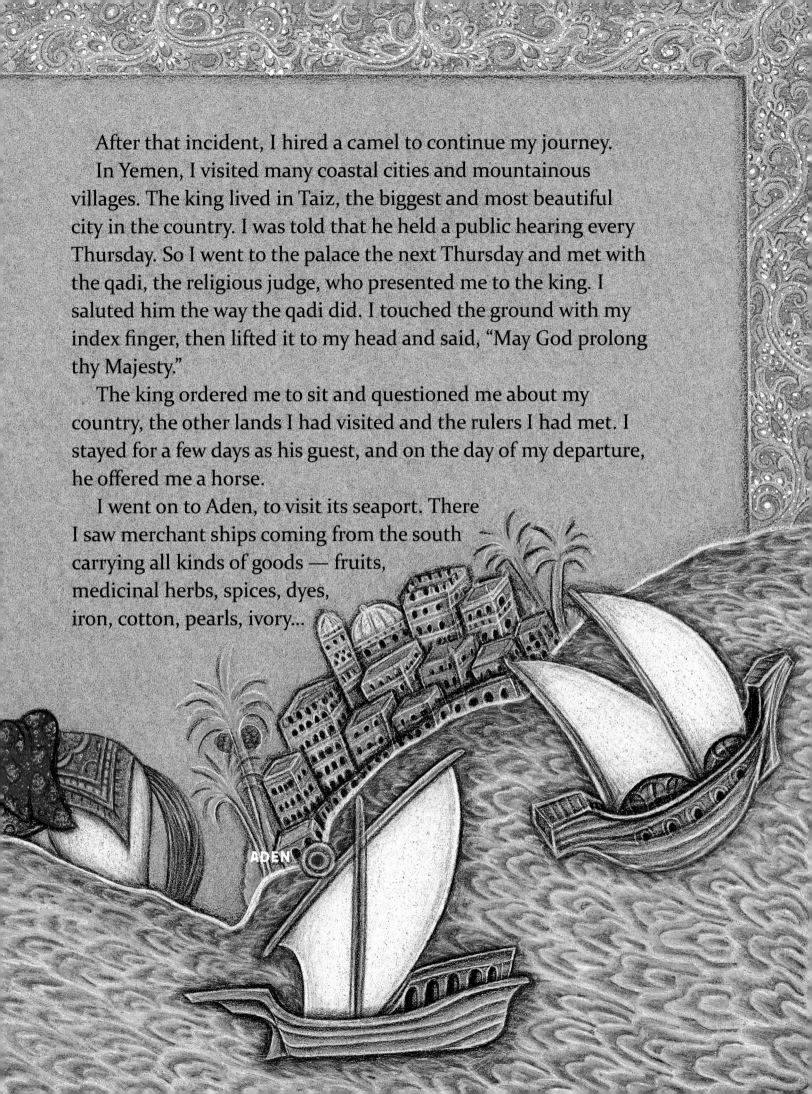

ADEN

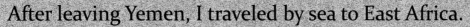

After leaving Yemen, I traveled by sea to East Africa.

At the port of Mogadishu, our ship was welcomed by a number of small boats. A man in each boat offered food in a covered dish to each of the merchants on the ship, saying, "Be my guest." Once on land, the merchants went to the homes of their hosts to exchange goods.

On Friday, the holy day, the qadi visited me with a gift — a new robe — then invited me to the mosque to pray behind the sheikh and the sultan. After prayers we went to the palace, where I stayed for a week.

When I rejoined the ship, we continued southwards. We ended up in the island town of Kilwa, in Tanzania, and stayed for fifteen days. We had to wait for the winds to change direction before we could sail north again.

MOGADISHU

KILWA

In 1332, I returned to Mecca, then traveled to Egypt and Syria, and then on to Anatolia, or Turkey. In Constantinople, I saw an amazing church built by the Greeks called Hagia Sophia. I also had the chance to meet theologians and governors there.

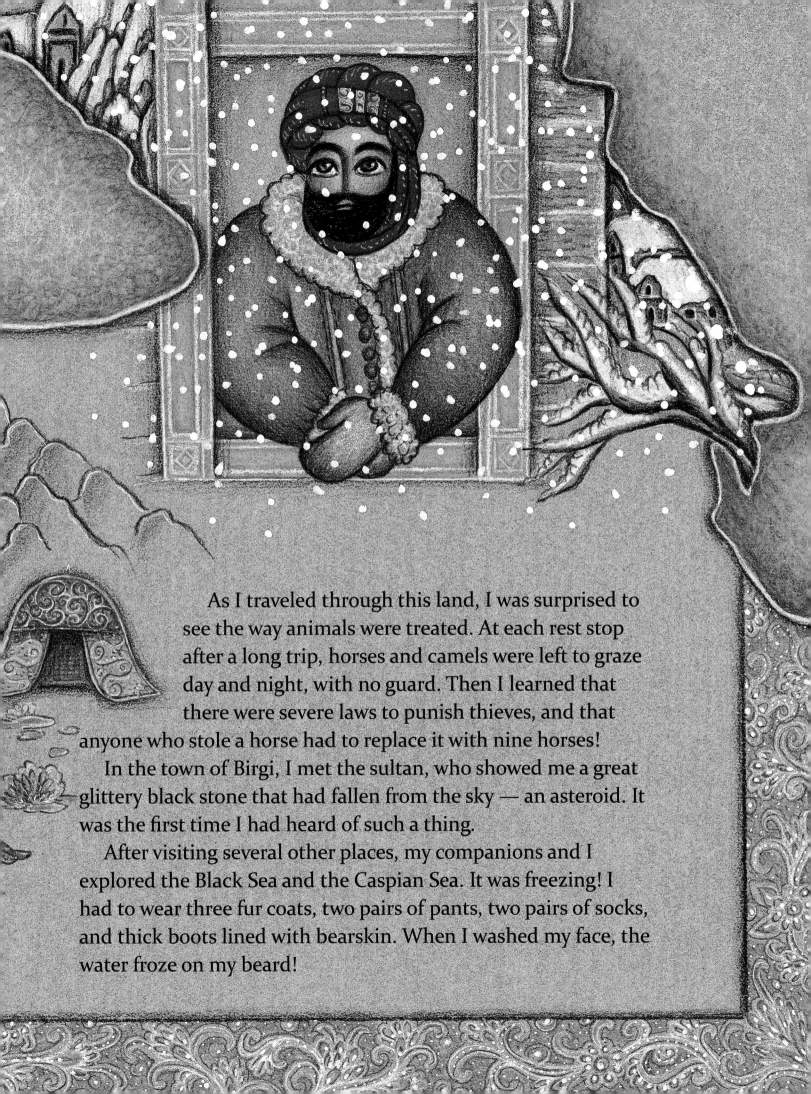

As I traveled through this land, I was surprised to see the way animals were treated. At each rest stop after a long trip, horses and camels were left to graze day and night, with no guard. Then I learned that there were severe laws to punish thieves, and that anyone who stole a horse had to replace it with nine horses!

In the town of Birgi, I met the sultan, who showed me a great glittery black stone that had fallen from the sky — an asteroid. It was the first time I had heard of such a thing.

After visiting several other places, my companions and I explored the Black Sea and the Caspian Sea. It was freezing! I had to wear three fur coats, two pairs of pants, two pairs of socks, and thick boots lined with bearskin. When I washed my face, the water froze on my beard!

From there I joined a caravan traveling to India, where it was much warmer. I was introduced to the sultan of Delhi, whom I entertained with my endless stories and knowledge. He asked me to stay and become the judge in his palace. After ten years, he made me the ambassador of India in China.

When I reached the seaport of Quanzhou, I was amazed to see that even the poorest people in China wore silk. They also had porcelain pottery decorated with the finest artwork. I was even impressed by the hens, which were bigger than the geese in my country!

GRANADA

In 1346, I decided to return to Mecca. On my way, I heard from caravan traders in Damascus that my father had died fifteen years before. That made me very sad.

I continued on to Mecca, but
it was a long and difficult journey
since a terrible deadly disease — the
plague — was infecting people in many
countries. There was death all around me.
Luckily, I did not get sick, but I felt the need to
go home. By then I was forty-five years old and
had been traveling for twenty-four years.

When I finally arrived in my hometown, Tangier,
I learned that my mother had died several
months before. I was so sad and wished I had
come back earlier.

I decided to travel again, this time to the Islamic
kingdom of Granada, in Spain. I was very impressed with
the beauty of the land and architecture, especially the
Alhambra, a palace and fortress surrounded by the loveliest
garden I had ever seen.

My last trip was to the Kingdom of Mali. I headed south
with a caravan going through the great desert, the Sahara.
The trip lasted several years and allowed me to learn about
numerous countries and cultures.

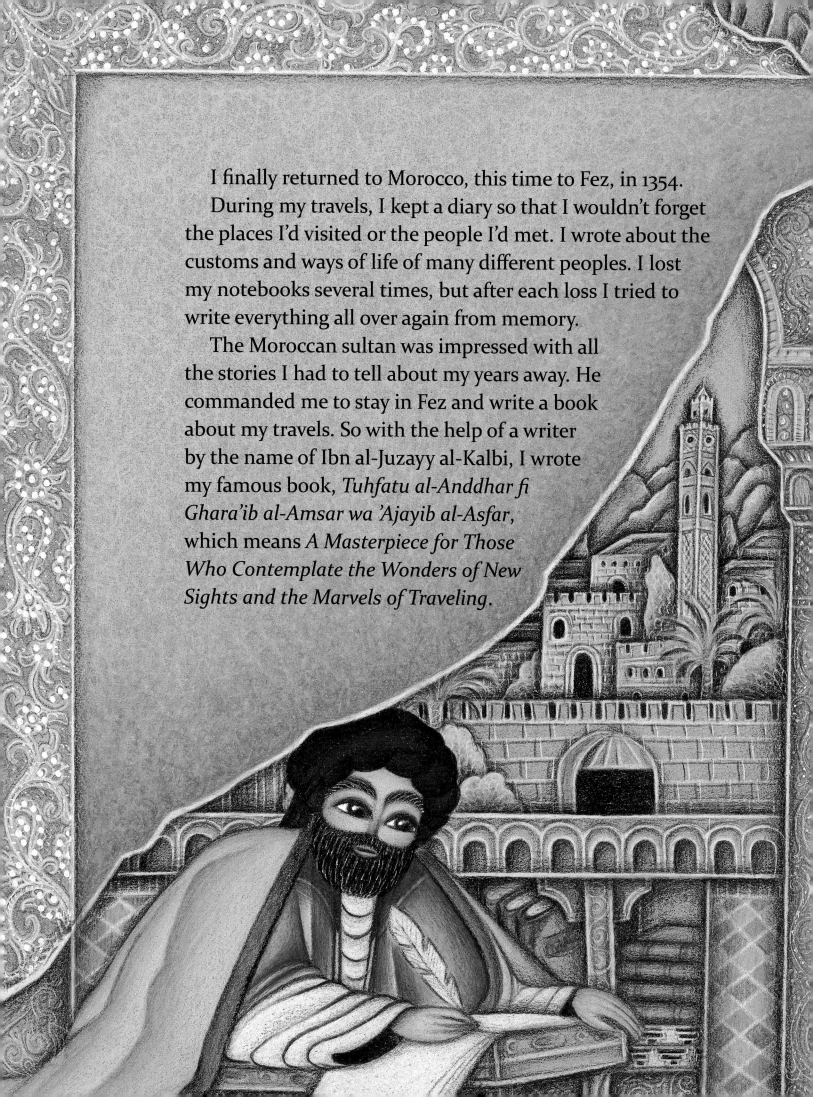

I finally returned to Morocco, this time to Fez, in 1354.
During my travels, I kept a diary so that I wouldn't forget
the places I'd visited or the people I'd met. I wrote about the
customs and ways of life of many different peoples. I lost
my notebooks several times, but after each loss I tried to
write everything all over again from memory.

The Moroccan sultan was impressed with all
the stories I had to tell about my years away. He
commanded me to stay in Fez and write a book
about my travels. So with the help of a writer
by the name of Ibn al-Juzayy al-Kalbi, I wrote
my famous book, *Tuhfatu al-Anddhar fi
Ghara'ib al-Amsar wa 'Ajayib al-Asfar*,
which means *A Masterpiece for Those
Who Contemplate the Wonders of New
Sights and the Marvels of Traveling.*

After my book was completed, I started to work as a
judge, helping resolve people's disputes and spreading
the knowledge and wisdom that I had gained through
my exploration of the world.

FEZ

Author's Note

As a writer for children and young adults, I see it as my duty to introduce them to prominent historical figures from the Arab and Islamic world — people who have contributed a great deal to shaping modern times in various scientific and literary fields.

I chose to start these biographical books with Ibn Battuta, a great traveler from the fourteenth century whose life has intrigued me since I was a child myself. I have used the first person so that the text seems autobiographical, and therefore closer to the reader.

Even though Ibn Battuta left behind manuscripts that describe his travels, gaps in the historical records make it difficult to account for all the details of his life. Historians know little about him after he returned to Morocco, except that he died at the age of sixty-five in 1369.

Ibn Battuta's manuscripts were gathered in a book commonly referred to as the Rihla (Journey) of Ibn Battuta. Five manuscripts of the Rihla can be found in the Bibliothèque nationale de France in Paris. Another manuscript is conserved in the John Rylands Library at the University of Manchester, and another at the Biblioteca Apostolica Vaticana in Vatican City.

Fatima Sharafeddine

Copyright © 2014 by Fatima Sharafeddine
First published in 2010 in Arabic as *Ibn Battuta* by Kalimat,
P.O. Box 21969 Sharjah, United Arab Emirates www.kalimat.ae
Copyright © 2010 by Fatima Sharafeddine

Published in 2014 by Groundwood Books / House of Anansi Press
groundwoodbooks.com
Fourth printing 2022

We gratefully acknowledge the Government of Canada for its financial support of our publishing program.

With the participation of the Government of Canada
Avec la participation du gouvernement du Canada

Library and Archives Canada Cataloguing in Publication
Sharafeddine, Fatima, author
The amazing travels of Ibn Battuta / by Fatima Sharafeddine ;
pictures by Intelaq Mohammed Ali.
Issued in print and electronic formats.
ISBN 978-1-55498-480-0 (bound). —
ISBN 978-1-55498-481-7 (html)
1. Ibn Batuta, 1304-1377 — Juvenile literature. 2. Travelers —
Islamic Empire — Biography — Juvenile literature. I. Ali,
Intelaq Mohammed, illustrator II. Title.
G370.I2S43 2014   j910'.92   C2013-905623-8
2013-905624-6

The illustrations were done in color pencil.
Printed and bound in Canada